STUDY GUIDE

UNSPOKEN

JOHNNY HUNT

HARVEST HOUSE PUBLISHERS
EUGENE, OREGON

UNSPOKEN STUDY GUIDE

Copyright © 2018 Johnny Hunt
Published by Harvest House Publishers
Eugene, Oregon 97408
www.harvesthousepublishers.com

ISBN 978-0-7369-7362-5 (pbk.)
ISBN 978-0-7369-7363-2 (eBook)

Printed in the United States of America

17 18 19 20 21 22 23 24 25 26 / BP-SK / 10 9 8 7 6 5 4 3 2 1

CONTENTS

How to Use This
Study Guide

In the introduction to my book *Unspoken*, I shared that my goal for writing the book—and this study guide—is that you'll grow in your understanding of who you are and who you can be. True satisfaction comes from becoming the men, the husbands, the fathers, the leaders that God made us to be.

The observations, questions, and prayers in this study guide are designed to help you take steps forward in making that happen. Within these pages are opportunities for you to experience real change, real growth.

While it's possible to use this study guide on your own, my hope is you will seek out other Christian men so that you can learn together, encourage each other, and build up one another. God designed Christians to function together. As Hebrews 10:24 says, "Let us consider one another in order to stir up love and good works." Growth happens as we interact.

More importantly, it is in the context of male friendships that life's challenges become more manageable. Whatever our struggles, they become easier to face when one or more others come alongside to offer a word of counsel or hope. Galatians 6:2 commands us to "bear one another's burdens." By going through this study guide with another man or in a group, you'll discover you're not alone in life's battles—and that there is strength in numbers.

My prayer is that you'll find yourself growing toward Christlike maturity as you make your way through this study guide, and that you'll become more and more the man God desires you to be.

Pastor Johnny

PART 1:

WHAT KEEPS US SILENT

The Silence of the Rams

THE MAIN IDEA

In general, men don't like to talk about issues that make them uneasy. This is especially true about their inner frustrations or struggles.

1. What are some of the things men find it difficult to talk about?

2. What are some reasons men find it difficult to talk about these things?

3. What are some of the negative consequences we can experience when we refuse to communicate our struggles and needs to others?

4. What are some of the positive results that can come from a willingness to speak up when we're inclined to stay silent?

FROM THE BOOK
UNSPOKEN

"Only heaven will reveal the problems, troubles, heartbreaks, and difficulties that have come our way as a result of our inability or unwillingness to speak what we'd rather leave unspoken."

1. In what ways can a failure to communicate have a negative impact on our relationship with God?

2. In what ways can a reluctance to communicate have a negative impact on...

- our marriage relationship?

- our family relationships?

- our work relationships?

- our church relationships?

"What we speak, as well as what we refuse or neglect to say, reveals a great deal about the condition of our heart."

1. Do you agree with that statement? Why or why not?

2. If our words are shaped by the condition of our heart, what does that say about the importance of having a heart that is right with God?

3. What are some ways you can make sure your heart is right with God?

The condition of your heart will determine how your life turns out—and a very close connection exists between your heart and your mouth.

4. Psalm 119:11 says, "Your word I have hidden in my heart, that I might not sin against you." In what specific way is the psalmist preparing himself so that he doesn't sin?

5. Colossians 3:16 says, "Let the word of Christ dwell in you richly." What are some different ways you can increase your intake of God's Word so that it dwells in you richly?

6. As you grow in your intake of God's Word, what impact do you think that will have on your communication?

CLOSING THOUGHTS

1. What stood out to you most in chapter 1, and why?

2. What one or two action steps do you plan to take this week toward being more open in your communication?

FROM YOUR HEART TO GOD'S

Father, thank You for reminding me of Your desire for believers to interact with one another so that they might help, encourage, and equip one another. Help me to realize the importance of speaking up—of letting those close to me know when I am struggling or in need. And before I speak, may I yield my heart to You. Your Word says, "Out of the abundance of the heart the mouth speaks" (Matthew 12:34). May I give greater priority to having a right heart… so that I will speak the right words.

2

Break the
Chains of Fear

THE MAIN IDEA

Fear is a major reason we stay silent when we should speak up. And fear can strike from a number of different directions. Perhaps we're ashamed of some hidden habit in our life. Or we don't want to ask questions or express a need because we're determined to be self-sufficient. Or we assume we're the only one struggling, and we don't want to look weak in front of other people.

Whatever the reason, you can be sure of this: The more you keep your fears to yourself, the more pleased Satan is. The enemy of your soul knows that when you stay quiet, you're more likely to become frustrated or discouraged. And you're more likely to lose your enthusiasm for the things of God.

The opposite is true as well: The more you're willing to speak up, the more likely it is that you'll be comforted, encouraged, strengthened. The more likely it is you will stay in God's Word, avoid succumbing to temptation, and be available to help others who are struggling.

1. Read James 5:16. What commands are given in this verse?

2. What does this passage have to say about prayer?

3. How have you felt in the past when you knew that someone was praying, on your behalf, about a specific need in your life?

4. If another man asked you to pray for him about a struggle he's facing, how would you respond, and why?

FROM THE BOOK
UNSPOKEN

"A high percentage of the men I know who keep silent about the crucial issues of their lives—issues that really demand discussion, or even confession—keep quiet because they fear the consequences of speaking up."

1. On page 28 of *Unspoken*, a list of possible consequences appears:

   - Loss of relationship (spouse, friends, family, business associates)
   - Loss of possessions (house, car, inheritance)
   - Loss of influence
   - Loss of comfort
   - Loss of reputation
   - Loss of employment
   - Loss of power
   - Loss of control
   - Loss of privilege
   - Loss of status

   Can you think of other consequences in addition to those that appear on the list?

2. We can't let our fear dominate us. When we look for someone to speak to, what qualities should we look for—qualities that will help reduce our fear?

3. Before you speak to another person, you'll want to speak to God first. What promise does James 1:5 offer in this regard?

"As we bring our 'covered' secrecy into the light, our dear Lord exposes it for what it is. At last, we become capable of seeing and admitting the ugly—but bondage-breaking—truth. When we bring that secret into the light, fear loses its power to keep us in slavery."

1. Can you share, from personal experience, about the freedom that came from bringing a secret into the light? What happened, and what positive results came from your confession?

Our heavenly Father intends to make us like His Son, Jesus Christ, who delights to do His Father's will. That is why our Lord frequently gives us time to choose to come clean.

2. Read Psalm 32:3-4. What happened when David kept silent about his sin?

3. Now read Psalm 32:7, 10. What happens to the person who trusts God?

"The enemy would have you believe that living a lie is better than the truth, but Jesus insists that only the truth has the power to set you free."

1. Do you believe that God is bigger than your guilt? That His mercy and grace are able to cover that which you've tried to hide? What evidence of His abundant mercy and grace have you seen elsewhere in your life?

2. In what ways did God show His mercy and grace to some of the people in Scripture? Try to come up with four or five examples.

CLOSING THOUGHTS

1. What stood out to you most in chapter 2, and why?

2. Christ died on the cross to deal with our sins and cleanse us. In doing that, He also dealt with the shame that comes with sin. Take time now to yield your sins and shame to God, and ask Him to give you the freedom that comes from having a clear conscience.

FROM YOUR HEART TO GOD'S

Lord, I am reminded of when the apostle Paul asked for Your help in the midst of a major challenge. You lovingly responded, "My grace is sufficient for you, for My strength is made perfect in weakness" (2 Corinthians 12:9). I believe Your infinite grace can cover my struggles, and so I offer up my weakness to You. Thank You for the mercy and grace You have poured out upon me through what Jesus did on the cross. He took my sin and shame so that I might know freedom. You didn't hold anything back when You showed Your love for me; may I not hold anything back from You.

3

PRIDE: THE ULTIMATE PATH TO SELF-DESTRUCTION

THE MAIN IDEA

One of the most potent forces keeping Christian men's mouths shut is pride. Rather than speak up and take a chance on being embarrassed or perceived as a failure, they'll stay silent.

Men are competitive and like to be perceived as winners. So anything that admits to a weakness, a problem, is swept under the rug. It's hidden.

Pride also keeps us from ever admitting when we're wrong. Remember what happened in the Garden of Eden? When God approached Adam after he had eaten the forbidden fruit, what did Adam do? He blamed Eve—"The woman whom You gave to be with me, she gave me of the tree, and I ate" (Genesis 3:12).

If we want to be the men God has called us to be, then we need to do away with pride and stop playing the blame game. Only then will we truly be winners.

1. How would you define pride?

2. How would you define humility?

3. What does God say about pride and humility in the following verses?

   • Proverbs 11:2—

   • Proverbs 13:10—

   • Philippians 2:3—

   • James 4:6—

   • James 4:10—

4. Do you agree that pride divides people, whereas humility unites them? Why would that be the case?

FROM THE BOOK
UNSPOKEN

"Note how God's Word contrasts human pride with God's wisdom, and how pride causes a man to close his ears to what God says: 'Where there is strife, there is pride, but wisdom is found in those who take advice' (Proverbs 13:10 NIV)."

1. Can you think of some specific ways that pride might cause a man to "close his ears to what God says"?

2. Proverbs 13:10 says, "Wisdom is found in those who take advice." Why is a willingness to accept advice a good thing?

"Pride not only stops up a man's ears, it also shuts down his heart... We were made for fellowship with God, but pride makes that fellowship impossible."

1. To put this into perspective, imagine a child who is too proud to listen to his parents. In what ways might that child's pride hurt his relationship with his mom and dad?

2. Can you think of a time when pride interfered with your relationship with God? What happened, and what did you do to restore an open relationship with God?

Proud men can be very religious, but they cannot be godly.

"Much of the time, a proud man doesn't suffer from a lack of information, but from intense personal resistance to the information he already has."

1. Often when we hide sin in our hearts, we know exactly what we're doing and just don't want to admit it. Ultimately this means you have to ask yourself: Do I love this sin more, or do I love God more?

   • What are the evidences that indicate a person loves sin more?

   • What are the evidences that indicate a person loves God more?

2. Read John 14:15, 23. What will the person who loves God do?

CLOSING THOUGHTS

1. When you see pride in another person, do you find it attractive or repulsive? Why?

2. What are some ways you can make sure pride doesn't gain a foothold in your heart?

FROM YOUR HEART TO GOD'S

Lord, help me to examine myself honestly—to see whether I've allowed pride to creep in unawares and close my ears and my heart to Your words. As a fallen person, I realize I'm inclined to become prideful. And it doesn't help that I live in a fallen world where pride is considered acceptable and even desirable.

May I follow Jesus's example of humility—seeking to put You first in everything, and to put the needs of others before my own. Your Word says that a wise man is willing to receive advice. May I be willing to receive the counsel You give to me through Scripture.

PART 2:

WHERE SILENCE IS KILLING US

4

Brain Ruts

THE MAIN IDEA

The statistics speak for themselves. Pornography is rampant today. And sadly, it's made deep inroads into the Christian community.

The very fact that Christian men who view pornography feel ashamed of their viewing habits says something as well. They're feeling guilty, but apparently they're not feeling convicted enough to try to do something about it. Or, maybe they've already made earnest efforts to come clean, only to succumb to temptation again…and again. And they've given up.

That pornography is such a struggle means it ought to be taken seriously. While we would much rather not say anything, making ourselves accountable to another spiritually mature man or two really can help make a difference. When we enlist others to help us in the task of guarding our mind—and of keeping our heart with all diligence—we discover that there truly is strength in numbers.

While we will never achieve perfect holiness for as long as we live on this earth, the Christian life is to be lived as a pursuit of Christlikeness. So when you feel convicted, yield yourself completely to the guidance of the Holy Spirit, who speaks through God's Word. As Romans 12:2 says, offer up your body as a living sacrifice, acknowledging that it belongs to God, and it's no longer your own.

And while temptations will continue to present themselves for as long as you live, don't grow weary in the face of them. Instead, take heart in the promise God gives in 1 Corinthians 10:13: "No temptation has overtaken you except such as is common to man; but God is faithful, who will not allow you to be tempted beyond what you are able, but with the temptation will also make the way of escape, that you may be able to bear it."

God is faithful, and He will help you.

FROM THE BOOK
UNSPOKEN

"Statistics tell us that a huge percentage of Christian guys...consume pornography at basically the same rates and levels as non-Christians..."

1. What message does a nonbeliever receive when he hears that Christian men view pornography at the same levels as non-Christians?

2. When Christian men engage in pornography to this extent, what impression might it give non-Christians about God and Christianity?

"Let's get honest...God created us with our sexuality. God created it for good, for pleasure, for procreation. But we have to get a handle on it."

1. Hebrews 13:4 says, "Marriage should be honored by all, and the marriage bed kept pure, for God will judge the adulterer and sexually immoral" (NIV). Why do you think God feels so strongly about the marriage bed being kept pure?

2. Jesus said, "You have heard that it was said, 'You shall not commit adultery.' But I tell you that anyone who looks at a woman lustfully has already committed adultery with her in his heart." Why would God see "mental adultery" as being equivalent to physical adultery?

3. What are some ways we can "get a handle" on our sexual desires?

The sobering truth is that what you put into your mind, you will act out and ultimately become.

"Pornography erodes your confidence and self-worth—it makes you feel lonely...An addiction to pornography makes you feel shame and self-condemnation."

1. Do you agree with that assessment of pornography's impact on a person? Why or why not?

2. When Adam felt ashamed about eating the forbidden fruit in the Garden of Eden, what did he do, according to Genesis 3:8? Why did he feel shame?

3. What does shame do to our relationship with God?

4. When we abstain from pornography, what effect would that have on our relationship with God? And with other people?

CLOSING THOUGHTS

1. In Psalm 119:37, David prayed, "Turn away my eyes from looking at worthless things, and revive me in your way." What does it mean to "turn away" your eyes from "worthless things" as you go about in everyday life?

2. Job said, "I made a covenant with my eyes not to look lustfully at a young woman" (Job 31:1 NIV). Do you think that making an actual commitment can help you in your resolve to abstain from pornography? And do you think that your resolve could be strengthened by including accountability to another Christian man or two? Why or why not?

FROM YOUR HEART TO GOD'S

Father God, as I ponder the lessons of this chapter, I am reminded of why Jesus died for my sins. He died to set me free from sin—to show me the way to redemption and forgiveness. Sin leads to shame and hiding; a rejection of sin leads to a clear conscience and joy. Satan wants me in bondage; You want to me to experience freedom.

When it comes to battling pornography and sexual temptation, I realize I need to call in reinforcements. I need to call upon You to provide a way of escape, which You promise to provide. I need to call upon the Holy Spirit to convict me so that I might repent and follow after You. And I need to call upon other men so that we can uphold one another in prayer and encouragement.

Thank You, Lord, for caring about my purity so much. For when I am pure, I am able to live the Christian life to the fullest, and enjoy the freedom that comes from a clear conscience.

5

A WISDOM CALL

THE MAIN IDEA

The matter of drinking is not an easy one to address. First there's the fact that wine in biblical times was different from the wine that's produced today. And there are differences of opinion as to where the line should be drawn in terms of what's appropriate for a Christian to drink.

What we do know for certain is that the Bible prohibits drunkenness. We also know the Bible speaks about the negative effects of alcohol consumption—for example, Proverbs 23:29-30 says, "Who has woe? Who has sorrow? Who has contention? Who has complaints? Those who linger long at the wine." And from everyday experience, we can see that alcohol can change a person's behavior. Then there are the statistics about alcohol-related injuries and deaths.

As the title of this chapter says, this is "a wisdom call." Taking what we know both biblically and factually, what principles would help a Christian man to make the best choices with regard to drink? In Ephesians 5:18, we are exhorted to "be filled with the Spirit" and "not be drunk with wine." What are we allowing our mental, emotional, and physical faculties to be controlled by?

FROM THE BOOK
UNSPOKEN

"While guys typically have no problem speaking about what they call drinking 'recreationally' or 'in moderation,' they get very quiet indeed when their drinking habits start to shift. Did you know that the top two signs of problem drinking both involve secrecy?"

1. Regardless of whether or not you drink any alcoholic beverages, why is it that someone who is on the path to problem drinking would want to hide the evidence for that?

2. When we attempt to hide a behavior, is that a silent way of admitting something might be wrong? What are we doing to ourselves when we become secretive about any habits present in our life?

"I doubt I can say it any better than did a friend of mine, Josh Franklin: 'I will argue against drinking alcohol as a beverage...However, I know that there are those who disagree with me. They may feel that they have Scripture to support their moderate drinking. I do not have the right, nor does any other Christian, to look down my nose in a judgmental manner toward someone who is struggling to be free or for one reason or another does not feel that Scripture condemns the practice...[One's stance on alcohol] is not what we'd call a top-tier doctrine of our faith and practice as believers."

1. In light of the words above, what seems to be a reasonable "balance" for Christians to have when it comes to a person's choice about whether to drink or not?

2. Galatians 5:13 says, "For you, brethren, have been called to liberty; only do not use your liberty as an opportunity for the flesh, but through love serve one another." What do you see as the primary admonishment in this verse?

"What about your influence on others? In your home, at work, at school, you can influence others for good or for ill."

1. Today's culture says, "Do whatever you want. If it feels good, do it." But according to Philippians 2:3-4, what mindset are we to have?

2. A little later, in Philippians 2:14-15, what additional exhortation are we given?

3. When it comes to your influence on others, how would you want other people to describe that influence?

CLOSING THOUGHTS

1. Read the following verses, and after each one, write what God desires of you as a believer:

   • Matthew 6:33—

   • Ephesians 4:1-3—

   • Ephesians 4:22-24—

2. As you ponder God's desire for your life, does that influence your thoughts about living for yourself as opposed to living for others? In what ways?

FROM YOUR HEART TO GOD'S

Lord, when it comes to the matter of drink, help me to use careful discernment. May my thoughts and decisions be based on principles from Your Word, and not my own desires or what society says is okay. I want, above all, to yield to Your guiding influence in my life.

For when I do that, then I allow You to do Your work through me to those around me. May I follow Jesus's example of putting others first…so that they might be built up and encouraged, and You would be glorified.

6

The Pressure of Providing

THE MAIN IDEA

One very important way a man shows his love for his family is by providing for them. This seems to be an innate part of a man's identity—to the point that men very often evaluate themselves on the basis of how they are performing in this area.

The fact we live in a materially affluent society doesn't help. It puts the expectations higher. The gadgets that are part of everyday living continue to get more expensive. In a number of ways, it's getting harder and harder not just to get ahead, but to merely maintain whatever economic stature we've managed to reach.

And providing for one's family goes beyond just the money aspect. As the head of the home, a man is to oversee the spiritual needs of his wife and children. There's far more to that than going to church on Sunday—it's a seven-days-a-week occupation that requires intentional planning and care for the spiritual nurture and growth of each family member.

Then there are health and medical issues, home maintenance matters, and still other obligations. No wonder the pressure is so great!

FROM THE BOOK
UNSPOKEN

"Guys want to be good providers...From the very beginning, way back in the Garden of Eden, God gave man a job...To this day, men have a powerful, divinely implanted urge deep within them to work hard and take care of their families."

1. Do you agree with this assessment about men wanting to take good care of their families? Name two or three specific ways you experience fulfillment when it comes to providing for your wife or children.

2. How do you feel when, for some reason or another, it's beyond your ability to take care of a specific need?

3. Is there more you could do to involve God in your everyday efforts to provide? In what ways can you do that?

"If God considers a man the spiritual head of his home, what does that involve? Does he need to teach his children how to pray? How to read and study the Bible? How does he help lead them to a saving knowledge of Jesus Christ? What does it look like for him to lead his wife in spiritual matters?"

1. Would you say that providing spiritually for your family is even more important than providing economically? Why or why not?

2. In what areas could you improve in the spiritual care you provide?

3. What are some of the benefits that would result from doing a good job of providing for your family spiritually?

Whenever you find yourself under the massive pressure that often accompanies your responsibility to provide, God means for you to look up.

"We all have times when it feels as though everything we've worked for and labored to create might come crashing down upon our heads. We feel tired, weary, discouraged, disappointed, and maybe more than a little frightened—although we wouldn't dream of telling anyone any of that.

"But why not? How could it hurt to let someone else know the enormous pressure you feel? Wouldn't it actually be more beneficial to speak up to someone you can trust?"

1. Why do you think men are usually reluctant to tell anyone about the stresses they face in providing for their family?

2. In what ways might we benefit if we were to share our burdens with a trustworthy friend or two?

3. If another man were to come to you for help with the pressure he is facing, would you be willing to offer counsel to him? Why would a willingness to help be a win-win situation for both of you?

CLOSING THOUGHTS

1. What stood out to you most in chapter 6, and why?

2. Share about one or two specific ways that God has helped you in the past when you were under enormous pressure. What did you learn from those incidents?

FROM YOUR HEART TO GOD'S

Lord, You have told us to cast our anxieties upon You. And You have said that we are to worry about nothing, but in everything, give thanks.

As I provide for my family, help me to remember that ultimately, You are our provider. You have promised to care for Your own. Help me to trust in that promise, even when I cannot see the ways in which You will supply our needs. Rather than focus on that which seems to be lacking, remind me of the many blessings You have poured out upon us. You are the best provider we could possibly have.

7

I Need a Money Miracle

THE MAIN IDEA

When it comes to spending money, it's surprising how many people don't take the time to create a budget or at least plan ahead. Without a budget or advance planning, it's easy for us to be unaware of just how quickly our money is disappearing. When we don't keep track of our spending, we will usually end up in financial trouble.

What's remarkable is that setting up safeguards that help prevent money problems doesn't require a lot of time or effort. Much of it comes down to having the right mindset (everything belongs to God), and exercising discipline (know how much you make, set up a budget, and follow it). By contrast, it is monumentally more difficult to dig yourself out of a financial hole. So any steps you take right now—no matter what your situation—will get you started on the path to replacing your financial anxiety with peace.

FROM THE BOOK
UNSPOKEN

"I'm not suggesting that we broadcast to all comers about our money troubles. But neither does it help us to keep quiet about our problem and pretend as though it doesn't exist."

1. Why is it that money problems are so tough to talk about?

2. It's often said that one of the major reasons for marital disputes is disagreement over financial issues. What can a couple do to help diminish the likelihood of friction over money matters?

"Failing to plan is planning to fail...Do you keep a running track of all your expenses? Or do you just use your debit card to pay for everything from a single 'pot'?"

1. Why is it important to have architects draw up building plans? Why are recipes important for cooks? What are some other ways people prepare, in advance, for a project to be successful?

2. Once money is spent, it's gone, which makes it all the more imperative to put together a budget to keep track of your spending. Why do you think so many people won't take the time to do this? How many advantages can you come up with in favor of creating a budget?

Everything we have really belongs to God. We're simply stewards for a time, of His bounty. That's why we need to learn how to manage it well.

"Scripture speaks a great deal about money and our use of it, primarily because if we don't control the money that God puts into our hands, it will soon control us."

1. Knowing what the Bible says about money can have an impact on how we view it. What helpful principles do you find in the following verses?

   • Proverbs 3:9-10—

   • Matthew 6:19-21—

   • Matthew 6:24—

   • Hebrews 13:5—

2. Read Matthew 6:25-34. While this is a somewhat lengthy passage, the lesson Jesus teaches here is fairly simple. What do you perceive to be Jesus's main point?

3. At first glance, it may seem that if you have financial problems, you can't have inner peace. But for the Christian, it *is* possible. According to Philippians 4:6-7, how can you experience inner peace no matter what your external circumstances?

CLOSING THOUGHTS

1. What stood out to you most in chapter 7, and why?

2. What do you think would happen to your mindset about money if you took the time to seriously pray to God about (1) managing your money wisely on a daily basis, and (2) how you should proceed when it comes to major financial decisions?

FROM YOUR HEART TO GOD'S

Lord, You are the one who has made all things. Everything that I have comes from Your hand. Help me to remember I am merely a steward. My desire is to manage my finances and possessions wisely so that those around me can know You are a good and caring God.

While money is important, I don't want it to be a distraction. Help me to keep it in its proper place, and to control it instead of letting it control me. Any financial anxieties that are heavy on my heart right now, I give to You. May I put to work the principles that will help me be a good steward, and thank You for the inner peace You give to those who place their full trust in You.

8

My Wife Talks
Enough for
Both of Us

THE MAIN IDEA

Ultimately it doesn't matter whether women or men talk more. What counts is that communication itself takes place. Imagine a boss who doesn't communicate to employees. Or a military leader who doesn't communicate to soldiers. Or a parent failing to communicate what is expected of children.

It doesn't take much to realize that a lack of communication between people makes for weak or nonexistent links. And when that's the case, confusion or chaos will prevail. Good communication leads to good connection.

So what can we do to become better communicators?

FROM THE BOOK
UNSPOKEN

"We don't connect with our spouse more deeply by learning how to communicate more effectively. Rather, we start communicating better with our mate when we get back to connecting with her as we did at the beginning."

1. Why do you think "connecting" is such a crucial part of good communication?

2. What do you appreciate about your wife that makes you want to connect with her? What can you do to connect with her more, and not just communicate?

"When our Lord tells us, 'Husbands, love your wives, just as Christ also loved the church and gave Himself for her' (Ephesians 5:25), He's not making a mere suggestion. That's a command."

1. In what ways did Christ show His love for the church?

2. With that in mind, how can a husband show Christlike love to his wife?

3. What one way can you express that Christlike love to your wife today?

Once Spirit-filled surrender begins to take hold in my life, I will increasingly become a Spirit-directed person who is willing to sacrifice my own interests for the well-being of my wife.

"It's important that we husbands take time to pray with our wives. Through the years, I have tried to practice not only praying for my wife, but also praying with her."

1. What, ultimately, is the purpose of prayer?

2. Keeping in mind the answer to the question above, what benefits can you see in making a habit of praying regularly with your wife?

CLOSING THOUGHTS

1. What stood out to you most in chapter 8, and why?

2. Take time now to thank God for your wife, and come up with two or three specific ways you can connect with her this week.

FROM YOUR HEART TO GOD'S

Lord, thank You for the gift of communication. As I speak to others—and especially my wife—may I remember the importance of going beyond just words and making a genuine effort to listen, to empathize, to connect.

And thank You for Your example as a master communicator. You've spoken to us not only through Your perfect Word, but through Your Son, Jesus Christ, who spoke truthfully and lovingly. In these ways You've shown Your infinite wisdom and compassion, leading us to salvation and eternal life with You. These are the ultimate results of Your communication!

In all my communication with others, dear Lord, may "the words of my mouth and the meditation of my heart be acceptable in your sight" (Psalm 19:14 ESV).

9

Dump the Poison

THE MAIN IDEA

The greatest danger of bitterness is the way it buries itself deep within us if left unresolved. We might never talk about it—for days, weeks, months, or even years. But for however long you don't deal with it, you will feel negative effects in your life.

When bitterness takes residence in you, it affects your relationships. Mostly it affects any interaction you might have against the person you're angry at. But it can also strain your relationships with others who have nothing to do with the situation. And it most definitely hinders your relationship with God.

Why is that? Because bitterness impairs your ability to see life with 100 percent clarity. It impedes your spiritual growth. It inhibits your peace and joy. It stirs up attitudes within you that otherwise might not make an appearance.

In fact, Hebrews 2:14-15 makes it clear that bitterness causes trouble and defiles. First Corinthians 3:3 asks, "[When] there is jealousy and strife among you, are you not of the flesh and behaving only in a human way?" To behave "in a human way" means in a sinful way. As Christians, we're to put off our old thoughts, attitudes, and actions. Ephesians 5:8 says, "You were once darkness, but now you are light in the Lord. Walk as children of light."

Let's learn what it takes to deal with bitterness—and know freedom from it.

FROM THE BOOK
UNSPOKEN

"Ultimately we can't be bitter toward someone and still love Jesus as we ought. That means we must let go of our bitterness so we can be all that Jesus wants us to be."

1. Read John 15:4-5, Galatians 5:16, and 1 John 1:6. In what ways do these passages make it clear that holiness and sin are incompatible?

2. Again, based on the passages above, is it possible for us to abide completely in Christ and yet harbor bitterness in our hearts? Why not?

"Have you ever considered that in your bitterness, if you would just obey God and trust Him, that maybe you could move from a place of bitterness to an oasis? How far away might you be from an oasis right now?"

1. What are some of the reasons we find it so hard to let go of bitterness?

2. Read Romans 12:18-21.

    • How does verse 18 say we are to live?

    • What does verse 19 say about vengeance?

    • According to verses 20-21, how are we to treat our
      enemies?

3. Read Matthew 5:44. What command are we given here? Has
God allowed for any exceptions?

4. Why do you think God wants us to trust Him to deal with our
enemies?

God not only gives us truth, he gives us the power and the ability to obey that truth as we submit to His Spirit.

"If we are going to hear what God wants to speak to us, then we must open ourselves up to see what we might not want to see, whether in ourselves or in others."

1. When we hold onto bitterness, in a sense we're saying, "God, I don't want to listen to You." What is the danger of having that kind of attitude?

2. Imagine coming before God and letting go of bitterness. What good things can come from doing that?

CLOSING THOUGHTS

1. At the end of the chapter we are told three ways we can fight bitterness: with God's compassion, with His grace, and by admitting the truth and doing something about it. How much compassion and grace did God show to you when He forgave your sins and gave you salvation in Jesus Christ? Isn't it only right, then, to extend that same compassion and grace to others?

2. When someone hurts or harms us in some way, what can we do to prevent bitterness from taking root in our hearts?

FROM YOUR HEART TO GOD'S

Father, thank You for being so frank about bitterness in Your Word. Now I can understand why it is so damaging, and why it can affect even the relationships I have with good friends and with You.

Help me to examine my heart with brutal honesty and see if there is any anger, any resentment I need to deal with. Help me to realize how poisonous bitterness is, and why it's so necessary to let it go. Your Word clearly says I am to love and pray for my enemies. That's very hard to do, but I realize I need to surrender my bitterness, for You said that vengeance is Yours alone. You are the perfect and all-wise judge; help me to trust that You will do what is right. May I rest in Your justice, and not seek my own.

Finally, help me to guard my heart from allowing bitterness to take root in the first place. I don't want anything to hinder the freedom and joy I have in You.

10

There's Hope
for Depression

THE MAIN IDEA

Depression not only wants to pull you down; it also wants to isolate you from others. The only way depression can "stay alive" in you is by fending off any way for you to receive hope or encouragement. It wants you to think there is no way out, no chance of returning to normal.

Depression fogs the mind. It prevents you from seeing anything past your own inner world. And it plants doubts in your mind—doubts about yourself, about others, and particularly about God.

All of this makes it hard for you to "step outside" of your depression and see what you need to do to overcome it. That's why it's so important that you turn to God's Word and speak up to trusted friends when depression sets in. Both resources can offer—continually—the encouragement and hope you need so that eventually, you can emerge victorious.

Clinging to God's promises and reaching out to others—these are the cure to depression.

FROM THE BOOK
UNSPOKEN

"Depression...wants you to believe you have no chance to move beyond your current dark circumstance. It makes you fear that you'll never feel good again."

1. Can you name some people in the Bible who were in extremely difficult circumstances that may have seemed hopeless? What was their situation, and how did God come through for them?

2. We may experience times when we feel as though God has abandoned us, doesn't care for us, or won't hear our prayers. When that happens, what promise can we cling to in Hebrews 13:5?

3. Abraham and Sarah were 100 and 90 years old before God gave them a baby son. Moses hid in the wilderness for 40 years before God called him to lead the people of Israel out of Egypt. The people of Judah were captive in Babylon for 70 years before they were allowed to return to their homeland. The wait may be long, but God keeps His promises. What are some benefits we can gain from long waits before God comes through for us?

"Depression impacts every aspect of a man's life...spiritually, emotionally, mentally, physically, and relationally."

1. In light of that statement, how reliable do you think our feelings or thoughts are when we're in the midst of depression?

2. Why is it so important that we surround ourselves with trusted friends when we're depressed?

Someone cares for you; the cross of Jesus Christ proves it. Your future is not dim; the resurrection assures you of that.

"I confess that because of the darkness I went through, I'm a better husband. I'm a more compassionate pastor. I'm a better listener."

1. Can you give an example of a bad experience you went through, which, in the end, made you a better person?

2. Read 2 Corinthians 1:3-4. In what way can our suffering today be a good thing for others in the future?

CLOSING THOUGHTS

1. What stood out to you the most in chapter 10, and why?

2. Write down Hebrews 13:5 on a small card or piece of paper, and commit the verse to memory. Let it serve as a reminder to you that no matter how dark the night becomes, God has not abandoned you.

FROM YOUR HEART TO GOD'S

Lord, thank You for the many examples in Scripture of people who experienced despair or depression, yet in one way or another, they saw You come to their aid. The record of Your faithfulness in the past is my assurance of Your faithfulness in the future.

I know that no matter what happens, and no matter what my feelings tell me, You will not abandon me. While there is so much I don't understand about the difficulties I face in life, I know I can trust You completely. You are all-wise, and You are all-loving, and that won't change no matter how dark the night becomes. Thank You that I can rest in Your goodness.

11

IN THE
TORMENTOR'S HAND

THE MAIN IDEA

It seems ironic that a refusal to forgive someone else puts *you* in bondage—not the other person. While the other person may have done wrong, still, Scripture is very clear: We are to forgive in the same way God has forgiven us. Ephesians 4:32 says, "Be kind to one another, tenderhearted, forgiving one another, even as God in Christ forgave you."

It helps to remember the astounding truth in 1 John 4:19: "We love Him because He first loved us." When we were utterly lost in sin and darkness, God took the initiative to reach out to us. He extended His love first—He didn't want for us to clean up our act. As Romans 5:8 says, "God demonstrates His own love toward us, in that while we were still sinners, Christ died."

Similarly, even when we have been wronged, we are to take the initiative to love and forgive.

It's not easy. And it doesn't mean that restoration will necessarily take place. The other person might never apologize. But by forgiving and moving on, you free yourself from bondage—and you demonstrate the nature of God's forgiveness. You reflect the amazing extent of His love toward those who don't deserve it.

FROM THE BOOK
UNSPOKEN

"Your unwillingness to forgive will lead to a kind of personal torment you can't even imagine."

1. What are some ways we can end up hurting ourselves by refusing to forgive others?

2. By contrast, what are we likely to experience when we are willing to forgive?

"How much did Jesus forgive us at Calvary? We all owe to God a debt that is infinitely greater than 10,000 talents. None of us could ever repay it."

1. What thoughts go through your mind as you consider the forgiveness made available to you through Jesus?

2. When we refuse to forgive a specific offense, we are, in essence, saying that Jesus shouldn't be willing to forgive that offense either. Viewed from that perspective, is it *ever* right for us to withhold forgiveness? Why or why not?

God has called upon
all His children
to mimic His
willingness to forgive.
He intends it as a
hallmark of everyone
in His family.

"The Bible teaches us that forgiveness liberates. It frees us from a heavy load of guilt, bitterness, and long-harbored anger. Unforgiveness, by contrast, cripples your faith."

1. Can you share, from personal experience, about the liberating freedom that comes from forgiveness? What happened?

2. Imagine someone has wronged you. If the other person knows you are a Christian and you say you refuse to forgive him, what impression might that person get about God and Christians in general? By contrast, if you show forgiveness, how might that be a positive testimony?

CLOSING THOUGHTS

1. What stood out to you most in chapter 11, and why?

2. Is there someone you need to forgive? Take time now to release that person to God, and ask Him for wisdom about how to best move forward. Remember that offering forgiveness doesn't mean you expect reconciliation to take place. Nor does it mean you are denying that anything wrong took place. What it does mean is that you're letting go, and you're putting the matter into God's hands.

FROM YOUR HEART TO GOD'S

Lord, as I see how stubborn my heart can be sometimes, I stand in awe of Your infinite forgiveness, which You've made available to even the worst of sinners. What amazing love, what amazing grace!

Thank You for helping me to realize that when I withhold forgiveness, I am actually hurting myself more than I'm hurting the person who offended me. No matter how tempting it is for me to hold a grudge, I need to be willing to let go.

Convict my heart when unforgiveness resides in it. Give me the courage to do what is right—to forgive as You forgave. Help me to see my enemies through Your eyes—to see them as those who need Your love as much as I need it.

PART 3:

A Place to Untie Our Tongues

12

You Need More Male Friends

THE MAIN IDEA

When it comes to the issues men don't like to talk about, speaking up is the first step. But who do you speak up to? Where can you go to get wise counsel?

In the remaining three chapters of this study guide, we'll find the answers. We'll see the importance of male friends, coaches, and of making ourselves available to mentor others. It is in the context of these kinds of relationships that we gain the kind of support system that enables us to address life's battles head-on. Knowing that others are watching us—and we, in turn, are watching them—gives us a confidence and courage we would find much more difficult to summon when we're all alone.

Let's start by finding out about the kinds of male friends we need to surround ourselves with.

FROM THE BOOK
UNSPOKEN

"None of us have reached where we are on our own. It took friends to get us here."

1. Can you share about one or two ways that statement has proven true in your own life?

2. What qualities are most important to you when it comes to finding a good friend? Why?

"Do you have friends who can help you find strength in God, especially when your circumstances get dangerous, difficult, or nasty?"

1. Maybe you haven't given a lot of thought to cultivating male friendships with the idea that these men would help you in times of true need. What can you do to start building such friendships?

2. It's important to remember that true friendship is a two-way street. With that in mind, what are some ways *you* can become the right kind of friend to other men you know?

*This may be the
perfect day to draft
a letter or an email,
send a text or a gift,
or make a call to let
that friend know
the difference he has
made in your life.*

"Every man needs someone to love him, to pray for him, and to believe in him."

1. When you know that someone believes in you, what effect does that have on you?

2. In the same way that you need the affirmation and prayers of other men, you need to return the favor. Who can you be praying for right now, in what ways?

CLOSING THOUGHTS

1. Think about a man or two who, at some point in your life, was a true friend. Without mentioning his name or giving away too much personal information, explain why his friendship meant so much to you.

2. True friendship requires honesty. That means being willing to tell each other the truth even when it hurts. Why is such transparency important in a friendship?

FROM YOUR HEART TO GOD'S

Father, as I read about the importance of male friendships, may I not only seek out those men who can love me, pray for me, and believe in me; may I also be that kind of friend to others. In the same way that I have been blessed by others, I want to be a blessing to others.

Thank You, Lord, for the men You've used in my past to bring me to the point where I am today. In Your perfect wisdom, You knew what I needed, and when I needed it. I have experienced the incredible riches of Your goodness through their lives.

And thank You most of all for the ultimate friend, Jesus Christ. I know that He is always near, and that He hears my every prayer. There's no better friend I could ask for.

13

You Need a Coach

THE MAIN IDEA

A good coach can make a real difference in the direction a team takes over the course of a season. His style may inspire players in a way that compels them to crank their efforts up a notch, or it may rub them the wrong way, producing frustration and poor performance. That's why sports teams are willing to pay a premium for the best coaches—because their influence may mean the difference between just another season and going to the playoffs or even winning the championships.

In the Bible, we find many actual examples of coaching, Jesus and His disciples, and the apostle Paul and Timothy. Where would the disciples have been without Jesus? And where would Timothy have been without Paul? Pastors are called to equip those in the church. Spiritually mature men and women are urged to teach the younger men and women. Jesus commanded, "Go therefore and make disciples...teaching them to observe all things that I have commanded you" (Matthew 28:19-20). We all need a coach who can teach us as we seek to follow Christ.

Do you have a role model or two who can help you make better choices, wiser decisions, and reduce the number of missteps you take in life?

FROM THE BOOK
UNSPOKEN

"If the difference between winning a title and watching someone else win the title comes down to a good coach, then why wouldn't you willingly submit to his direction?...today a dizzying array of coaches have made themselves available in areas far beyond sports...you name the interest, there's probably a coach for it.

"Why is it, then, that in the most important area of life so few of us men even think about seeking out and working with a good coach?"

1. What are some reasons Christian men might not be more aggressive about seeking out good spiritual role models?

2. Is there a spiritual role model you've had in the past who has been helpful to you? Share the ways in which his example made a difference in your life.

"A good coach provides a healthy model of Christian conduct, a strong walk of faith, uplifting speech, and a focus on Christ. That's what you follow."

1. After reading the quote above, take a moment to write, in your own words, what each of these qualities would look like to you:

   A healthy model of Christian conduct—

   A strong walk of faith—

   Uplifting speech—

   A focus on Christ—

2. In your search for a coach for the Christian life, what are some additional characteristics you find helpful?

3. Imagine yourself as a coach to a man who is a new Christian. What are some things you would do to make sure you're adequately equipped to be a role model?

The simplest biblical definition of an effective coach may be what was written by the apostle Paul, who said, "Follow my example, as I follow the example of Christ"

(1 Corinthians 11:1 NIV).

"When it comes to good coaching, it's not so much what you hear a coach saying as it is what you see him doing. The big things are more often caught than taught."

1. Do you agree with the above statement? Why or why not?

2. Can you think about a time when a role model's action spoke louder to you than his words? Share about what happened, and what impact this had on you.

CLOSING THOUGHTS

1. Read Acts 20:18-24. How would you describe the kind of coaching Paul gave to the church leaders in Ephesus?

2. A little later in verse 27, Paul said, "I have not shunned to declare to you the whole counsel of God." In other words, if it appeared in Scripture, Paul taught it. He held nothing back. Why is this so important for a good coach to do?

FROM YOUR HEART TO GOD'S

Father, my heart is stirred as I realize just how much the concept of good coaching appears in Scripture. Your heart's desire is for those who are spiritually mature to raise up others toward spiritual maturity. In this way, Your church grows stronger and more capable of doing the work You have called it to do.

This helps me to realize all the more my own need for good role models in my life, so that I may follow them as they follow Christ. May I seek out those role models, and be diligent in applying what they teach me.

I've learned as well that this coaching thing works both ways—I need to make myself available to other men who can learn from me. Help me to develop the kind of walk of faith, uplifting speech, and focus on Christ that will prove uplifting to anyone who observes my life.

14

You Need a Colleague

THE MAIN IDEA

Everyone needs encouragement.

With all the challenges life throws at us, and given the fact we live in a fallen world filled with imperfect people who will say and do things that frustrate or discourage us, we can expect there will be times when we're down in the dumps. Worry, anxiety, and stress produce negative emotions in us. When plans don't work out or our circumstances spin out of control and there's nothing we can do about it, resignation or even depression can set in.

And unfortunately, in today's world, words intended to *discourage* are much more common than words intended to *encourage*. It seems as though the only way people know how to elevate themselves is to put others down.

What are the traits of an encourager so that we know one when we see one? And how can we, in turn, become encouragers to others?

FROM THE BOOK
UNSPOKEN

"The name Barnabas *means 'son of encouragement' in Hebrew...
Every man needs a Barnabas in his life—I do, and so do you. Who
do you go to when you need to share a burden, admit a failure,
talk over some worry, or float a trial balloon regarding one of
your ideas to see whether it's brilliant or crazy? Who will love and
respect you, but also tell you the truth without flinching?"*

1. What would you define as encouragement? And with
   that definition in mind, what would a person who is an
   encourager do?

2. What are some ways that encouragement benefits us?

3. In what areas of your life do you find you need
   encouragement most?

"God places people in our lives who are much wiser in certain areas than we are, and He sends them to us so they can give us counsel, lift our spirits, and provide encouragement when we need it."

1. If you find someone who, by nature, is an encourager, one way to develop an ongoing friendship is to seek him for advice. In what areas of your life could you use some advice right now?

2. Can you think of men who are qualified to provide input on those areas? Who are they, and what would you ask them?

Encouragers often play the role of "enlargers." They help you grow bigger, stronger, and more useful for the kingdom of God. They enlarge you.

"Members of the Clan of Barnabas are wonderful at encouragement, but all of them could use some encouragement of their own. Why don't you give it to them?"

1. Think of one or two men who have encouraged you in recent weeks or months. What simple thing could you do to show your appreciation for their help to you?

2. One lesson we can learn from encouragers is that they're generous with their wisdom and time. In what ways could you make an effort to be more generous to other men with your wisdom and time?

CLOSING THOUGHTS

Encouragers aren't the kind who are eager for the spotlight to shine on them. Instead, they're on the lookout for opportunities to lift up others. That's refreshingly different from the "What's in it for me?" attitude that's so rampant in today's culture. And if we're honest, because we're fallen humans, our tendency is, in fact, to be me-oriented.

With that in mind, below there is room to write two lists. In the left-hand column write down one-word descriptions that describe me-oriented people, and in the right-hand column, write one-word descriptions that describe other-oriented people (the list has been started for you with one example). After you finish writing the lists, ask yourself: In what two or three ways can I become more like an other-oriented person?

Traits of Me-Oriented People   **Traits of Other-Oriented People**

Selfish   *Generous*

FROM YOUR HEART TO GOD'S

Father, thank You for the example Barnabas set in Scripture—that he did what he could to lift others up and spur them onward in using their God-given talents. As I read Your Word in the weeks and months ahead, help me to see and learn from the other encouragers to be found in the Bible—Moses's father-in-law, Joshua, Nehemiah, Boaz, Mary, Paul, and others.

Lord, when other men take the time to encourage me, may I remember to express my appreciation to them, and may I take their words to heart. And when I see someone in need of encouragement, rather than hold back reluctantly, may I step forward and let You do the work You desire to do through me.

15

You Need a Colt

THE MAIN IDEA

One of the challenges of living the Christian life is that spiritual growth doesn't take place overnight. Day by day, week by week, month by month, we grow in imperceptible increments. But as time passes, slowly but surely we gain in stature, wisdom, and maturity.

We might think that we aren't really qualified to mentor other men until we no longer make mistakes, and we're cruising to the finish line. But the reality is, as long as we are on this earth, we will always have room to grow spiritually.

You don't need to wait until you are a "grandfather in the faith" to start coaching other men. There will always be men who are either new believers or haven't learned the lessons you've applied in your own life. A college student can mentor a high-schooler. A college graduate can provide guidance to a college student. A man with teens can counsel a man with newborns. A believer who has several years of steady spiritual growth can offer wisdom to those who are newer in the faith.

The options are many! God has gifted you with knowledge and experiences that would help others. Are you ready to make yourself available?

FROM THE BOOK
UNSPOKEN

"To become the fully mature man God calls you to be, you also need to learn how to build into the lives of other men. You need to become a mentor...and every mentor needs a young colt to train."

1. Have you ever taken time to assess the kind of knowledge and skills you can impart to others? Off the top of your head, try to think of two or three things you have to offer.

2. Think back to when you were in high school or college. Would you have felt awkward about approaching a more mature man and asking him to be a mentor? Why might a younger person or newer believer feel a bit reluctant to make such an inquiry? What can a prospective mentor do to communicate he is available to serve, and thus make it easier for a coach and colt to connect?

Mentoring is a process in which a more mature man chooses to get involved in the life of a less mature man in order to help him grow into the godly man God wants him to be.

"The main ingredient in mentoring is relationships. Mentoring isn't just saying, 'Come join my program.' It's about relationships, and relationships take time. They also can be inconvenient."

1. In what ways could a mentoring relationship be inconvenient?

2. What benefits can a mentoring relationship provide that help to offset any inconveniences that arise?

"Most real mentoring gets done in everyday living rather than in classroom settings."

1. Can you think of some examples of how a coach "handles everyday living" that might make a real impact on a colt?

2. What are some "everyday living" activities you can do with a colt that might be instructive to him?

CLOSING THOUGHTS

1. Think back to your growing-up years, when you were in
   school. Are there any specific memories that stand out to you
   in terms of their "learning value"? Share about what happened,
   and what you learned.

2. At the end of the chapter I say, "Pray that God will bring some
   good candidates into your life." That leads me to ask: How
   much do you involve God in your search for colts and your
   mentoring relationships? Why is it so crucial that we make
   God an active part of all we do when it comes to mentoring?

FROM YOUR HEART TO GOD'S

Father, as I come to You in prayer, I think about the ways I have grown because of men who took the time to mentor me, whether formally or informally. Thank You for their availability. Thank You for their heart for ministry and their willingness to equip me so that I can now pass along my wisdom and life skills to others.

As I seek to influence colts, remind me that my responsibility is not one to be taken lightly. In Scripture, You hold leaders to a high standard, with good reason. You call mentors to excellence so that those under them are in good hands. I realize that ultimately, I am accountable to You for the ways I invest myself in others. Help me to abide in You so that my life would represent, to a colt, how You desire for a Christian to live. May I seek, above all, to please You, and may the results of my coaching draw colts into a stronger relationship with You.

Speaking the Truth Will Set You Free

At the First Baptist Church of Woodstock, we have a ministry called The City of Refuge. The intent is to help those in the ministry who are faced with various types of struggles—marital problems, rebellious children, financial issues, the stress, and more.

The name *The City of Refuge* communicates, "Here is a place where you can find calm in the storm—where you can receive help and rest." We've had many wounded men and women come to receive counsel, encouragement, and answers for their problems.

In the epilogue to the book *Unspoken*, I share about a young pastor and his wife who came to The City of Refuge. At first, it appeared that it was the wife who was struggling and needed help. But as time went on, we came to realize it was the pastor who was dealing with significant sin issues, which, in turn, affected his wife.

It took a while for their issues to be resolved. It didn't help that the pastor, at first, was silent about his hidden sins. It wasn't until he had become transparent and honest that we were able to give them the counsel and help they needed.

My point is this: As long as sin remains hidden, it's impossible for change to take place.

That's why, when it comes to dealing with your struggles, it's vital for you to speak up. To be honest.

In chapter 3 of the book *Unspoken*, we looked at what happened to

King David when he kept silent after his adulterous affair with Bathsheba and his planned murder of her husband, Uriah. Let's look again at what David said:

> When I kept silent [about my sin], my bones grew old through my groaning all the day long. For day and night, Your hand was heavy upon me; my vitality was turned into the drought of summer (Psalm 32:3-4).

David's desperate efforts to keep his sins hidden affected him to the point that his body suffered physically. Perhaps you haven't felt similar effects in your own life, but there's no question that unconfessed sin is going to haunt you one way or another. You need to deal with it.

HOW SIN AFFECTS US

1. What are some examples of ways that hidden sin can affect our thoughts, feelings, and actions?

2. Read Proverbs 28:13.

   • What happens to the person who covers his sin?

   • What happens to the person who confesses his sin?

3. Why do you think God allows for us to experience negative consequences for our sins?

4. Why is it that when we struggle with sin, our tendency is to run *away* from God? Why is that a serious mistake?

THE EXTENT OF GOD'S LOVE AND FORGIVENESS

1. Going back to Psalm 32—according to verse 5, what happened when David admitted that he had sinned?

2. Read 1 John 1:9. What is God's response when we confess sin? How willing do you think God is to forgive us?

3. Read Ephesians 2:4-7:

> God, who is rich in mercy, because of His great love with which He loved us, even when we were dead in trespasses, made us alive together with Christ (by grace you have been saved), and raised us up together, and made us sit together in the heavenly places in Christ Jesus, that in the ages to come He might show the exceeding riches of His grace in His kindness toward us in Christ Jesus.

What specifically does this passage say about the extent of God's love for us, even when we were lost sinners?

4. Read 1 Peter 1:3-5:

> Blessed be the God and Father of our Lord Jesus Christ, who according to His abundant mercy has begotten us again to a living hope through the resurrection of Jesus Christ from the dead, to an inheritance incorruptible and undefiled and that does not fade away, reserved in heaven for you, who are kept by the power of God through faith for salvation ready to be revealed in the last time.

What does this passage say about the inheritance you have received as a result of salvation in Christ? Again, what does that tell you about God's love for you?

5. When you confess sin, you'll experience a clear conscience. Why is having a clear conscience such a positive experience?

CLOSING THOUGHTS

1. As you close out your time in this study guide, consider Jesus's words in John 8:32: "The truth shall make you free." In what ways would you say that being transparent—and truthful—really does set us free?

2. What two or three principles or lessons have meant the most to you in this study guide?

FROM YOUR HEART TO GOD'S

In the space below, write a prayer in which you express, to the Lord, your thanks for His love and mercy for you.

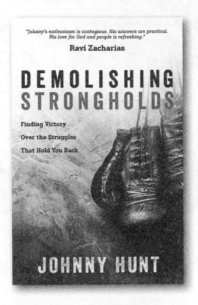

DEMOLISHING STRONGHOLDS

Ever wonder how to be a man of God in the trenches of life—in the day-to-day trials and temptations that hound you? It's not impossible! God's promises and strength are real, and you can claim them today.

Whether you feel beaten down by your past failures or trapped in a corner by your current struggles, let hope lift you up. Pastor Johnny Hunt offers the biblical encouragement and guidance that will help you...

- navigate the dangers and discouragements of daily life
- take practical steps toward taming your negative habits
- use your blessings to influence others for God's glory

It's time to learn how to break spiritual strongholds so you can move forward in God's will and become the kind of man you've always wanted to be.

To learn more about Harvest House books and
to read sample chapters, visit our website:

www.harvesthousepublishers.com

HARVEST HOUSE PUBLISHERS
EUGENE, OREGON